PERPETUAL MOTION GENIUS' GUIDE TO

Nathan Coppedge

PERPETUAL MOTION

GENIUS' GUIDE TO

INTERFACE DESIGN

Nathan Coppedge

FORE-NOTE

Nathan Coppedge

This guide was originally written as a component of another book titled The Dimensional Artist's Toolkit, in a section titled Synthetics. However, I have been meaning to write a text relating to the subject of interface design, not only because interface design is so prevalent and unrecognized in today's culture, but because I feel I have a lot of meaningful contributions to offer to this growing field.

This text begins by discussing a cup of tea. But understand, tea in my imagination has come to represent a symbol for the one-dimensional. Don't worry, some zazzy acronyms are in order by the end of this book, as I pursue interface design meaningfully up to the fifth dimensional standard.

Nathan Coppedge

GUIDE TO INTERFACE DESIGN

Nathan Coppedge

INTRODUCTION

The real experience of art may be summarized as the experience of experiences, a direction that is increasingly being followed in the media age. Art in the future will not exist without a science of the senses, and these senses will become chaotic if they are not subject to categories. Art will become chaotic, or the senses will have at least a superstition of regulation. Either regulation will be glorified, or chaos will be glorified.

Nathan Coppedge

1. THE CUP OF TEA

The first idea of the art object, according to synthesis, is the idea of a cup of tea. This is something to be enjoyed, which has an at first unpredictable sensation: bitterness. The substance is enjoyed through a paradoxical appreciation of its subtlety. It is at the same time, one quality, rather than several.

Nathan Coppedge

2. JAPANESE FOOD

Secondly, we have the idea of a row of small attached compartments. Each one contains a different type of food. The foods are all appreciated through a single lens, symbolized by chopsticks or some other utensil. What is appreciated is the variety, as well as the integrity of each category.

Nathan Coppedge

3. THREE-D SYNTHESIS

Thirdly, we move to the virtual age, and there are three dimensions of sensation. Instead of merely variety and integrity, we have variety and integrity and dynamic. This is part of the realization of the need for magical food and integrated experiences. One example of this is a cookie which is made artificially to remind us of majestic birds flying. Or a doorway which symbolizes, via our information (a secondary, simultaneously-running interface), that we have entered a secret level of knowledge. These types of examples are certainly dimensional, but they perhaps have not entered the ultimate level. What summarizes this level is association. To some extent this can be had without any hampering interface, except the natural body.

Nathan Coppedge

4. THE BEGINNING OF MEANING-FUL INTERFACE

Fourthly, we modify time to be more dimensional than previously. Instead of a linear structure of 'bits' such as secret tunnels in which we do or don't have information, or cookies which have the finite significance of a bird flying, instead, everything is rendered compoundable. This requires a degree of perfection and understandable complexity.

Now, if our knowledge is tainted by death, the cookie-bird dies, and if the cookie is NOT tainted by the knowledge (e.g. if we have a living knowledge), then we gain knowledge of birds when we eat the cookie. This is really a minimum standard, but it promises a wholly authentic reality which supplements technology. In this mode, levels could be gained every time a new experience is made available, provided that the new experience meets a symbolic quality standard (SQS). This level has been interrupted by the artificial desire for ready-made experiences (ADRME).

5. GENUINE USER INTERFACE (GUI)

Now enter the fifth level. Instead of objects modified by object-interactions (OMOI), we have objects created directly by user-input. Since user-input involves an appreciable degree of uniqueness and a remarkable degree of preference (ADURDP), objects are created with the standard of satisfying the user-entity (UE). Therefore, the entire standard of interface (SI) is based on the UE's ability to create a world.

Educated guesses are supplemented by knowledge-integration systems (KISs). A knowledge integration system may for example provide auto-customizable (e.g. through keywords or EEG) examples of user interface options (UIOs). Meaningful Existential Education (MEE) then depends on an ability to train the UE to build a world which satisfies his or her own curiosity and sense of meaning. A simple way to do this, for example, is to test for desirable works of art based on conceptual rules. Works of art can then be used as templates or razors for determining generally desirable experiences (GDEs).

With the right amount of study
and degree of computing complexity (DCC), there might be a desirable aesthetic for any chosen me-
dium, a universal aesthetic preference (UAP). However, the level of
complexification, perfection, and
interactivity produced in earlier
levels, and including this one,
should not be forgotten. The prop-
erties of the application must have
dedicated user functions (DUFs),
and user-customizable prefer-
ences (UCPs), preferably with EEG
capabilities or something more
advanced.

Nathan Coppedge

END-NOTE: ADDITIONAL DISCOV-
ERIES

Bear in mind that the concept of template or razor may be inclusive of logical and systematic structures which are themselves incorporated in interface. One recommendation, for example, is using exclusive categories in menu options (even in a visual diagram format), thus making menu categories into compoundable qualities (CQs), which can then be judged via a user-interface paradigm (UIP). Another paradigm is the toggle-click button which has not become widely available in UIs. Categorical organization would make such an option much more viable. There might even be codes or cognitive modifiers (CMs) upon click actions.

Nathan Coppedge

END
TRANSMISSION

Nathan Coppedge

Nathan Coppedge

BIO

Nathan Coppedge has been quoted in Book Forum and the Hartford Courant. He is a member of the International Honor Society for philosophy. He is the author of over thirty books.

www.ingramcontent.com/pod-product-compliance
Lightning Source LLC
Chambersburg PA
CBHW060936050326
40689CB00013B/3116